The End of Desire

Jill Bialosky

POEMS

The End of Desire

Alfred A. Knopf   New York   1997

Copyright © 1997 by Jill Bialosky

All rights reserved under International and Pan-American Copyright Conven-
tions. Published in the United States by Alfred A. Knopf, Inc., New York, and
simultaneously in Canada by Random House of Canada Limited, Toronto. Dis-
tributed by Random House, Inc., New York.

http://www.randomhouse.com/

Some of these poems originally appeared in the following magazines:

"The Goddess of Despair," under the title "Another Loss to Stop For," Section
8 from "Fathers in the Snow," *The New Yorker*

"Childbirth, 1943," "History Lesson," "Silver," "American Landscape," *PN Re-
view*

"My Groom," *TriQuarterly*

"The End of Desire," "The Dawn of the End of Civilization," *Seneca Review*

"The Lover's Gift," under the title "The Infidel's Gift," "Blueberries," *Gulfstream*

"Ruined Secret," "Stairway to Heaven," under the title "Ava Marie," *Agni Review*

"Carousel," *Pequod*

"Oh Giant Flowers," *Antioch Review*

"Cold Heart," *Partisan Review*

"Sisters," "Cornfields," "A Sister's Story," "Ballet Lesson," *International Poetry
Review*

"Without," *Intro 14*

Section 1 of "Fathers in the Snow," "The Game," "Skating Pond," *Pavement*

"Sisters" received the Elliott Coleman Award in Poetry, selected by Hugh Ken-
ner, and was published in *Ellipsis*.

"Oh Giant Flowers" was nominated for a General Electric Foundation Award.

Library of Congress Cataloging-in-Publication Data
Bialosky, Jill.
    The end of desire: poems / by Jill Bialosky.—1st ed.
       p.   cm.
    ISBN 0-679-45455-1
    I. Title.
PS3552.I19E53   1997
811'.54—dc20   96-43695
                                CIP

Manufactured in the United States of America
First Edition

AUG 1 2010

For my sisters, Laura *and* Cindy
and in memory of my sister Kim
and for my mother

and always to David *and* Lucas, *my sustainers*

I was of three minds,
Like a tree
In which there are three blackbirds.

Wallace Stevens

Contents

WINTER

The End of Desire

CORNFIELDS

Sometimes everything is clear:
men kneeling in cornfields,
where tall stalks surround them,
wives sorting laundry

that has breathed this air all day,
a child home from school
closing the books she will understand forever.

It is this time
when looking back is bearable.

Corn held small
in the farmer's large bruised hand
is all he really needs
when he looks out at dusk
over his long-worked field

and everything is yellow.

The House

The child's cry
Melts in the wall.

Sylvia Plath

FATHERS IN THE SNOW

In memory of Milton Abraham Bialosky

1.

The game is called *father*.

My sister lies in the grass.
I take handfuls of leaves
we raked from the lawn
spilling them over her body

until she's buried—

her red jacket lost, completely.
Then it's my turn.

Afterwards, we pick the brittle pieces
from each other's hair.

2.

After father died
the love was all through the house
untamed and sometimes violent.
When the dates came we went up to our rooms
and mother entertained.
Frank Sinatra's "Strangers in the Night,"
the smell of Chanel No. 5 in her hair and the laughter.
We sat crouched at the top of the stairs.
In the morning we found mother asleep on the couch
her hair messed, and the smell
of stale liquor in the room.
We knelt on the floor before her,
one by one touched our fingers
over the red flush in her face.
The chipped sunlight through the shutters.
It was a dark continent
we and mother shared;
it was sweet and lonesome,
the wake men left in our house.

3.

I'm not going to deny
the orange center of the flower
each last breath that passed
over the table
in the autumn gone away.

I wanted to take that afternoon
and put it in a safe place.
In a wooden box on the mantel
of a house I always imagine,
or in the hole I once dug
in the backyard for the imagined, stilled heart.

I wanted the day to stop
the way a movie would—
or to play it over in a place
my mind makes room for.

It was no large matter
of love, it was everything:
the grey afternoon, the Saturday
that began like a procession
inside a small flower
a young girl might tear apart.

4.

The day mother hammered closed
its silver door
we were outside
shaking the branches,
holding hands and dancing
in a circle around the tree.

Later, from the upstairs bathroom
we listened, three sisters taking turns.
One sister put her head
inside the laundry chute
that led through the deep tunnel
to the cellar,
called his name
and waited for the hollow echo
to answer back.

At night I faced the window,
my gold pillow, like a treasure,
pressed against my chest,
the giant tree spreading
over the house.

If I stared long enough
the branches would save me
from the voice of my father
trapped inside the chute.

5.

When the lightning
struck we were sure the dark limbs would splinter
but instead the tree was all light
and beautiful.
The tree long ago had been transformed,
had become for us, our father.

For days after the storm
we guarded its dark secret.
There were no blessings
large enough for that body
wrapped in weathered bark.

The day the men came
to cut down our tree
we had said them all:
One sister rubbed
her doll's face with mud
that covered the twisted roots,
the other sister hammered
her fist against the bark.

I carried a last leaf
in my pocket for luck.

6.

I come home
to the white framed house,
the paint on the side peeling
as if grieving for something lost

and the yellow forsythia tree
grown wild in the backyard
letting go its closed blossoms.

By the side door
is the milk chute
we crawled through
nights locked out of the house.

And in the backyard,
the stump of our oak tree
standing like a headstone
in the middle of the dried lawn.
Once its brown limbs protected our roof.

Indoors mother sleeps
all day on her double bed
while dandelions work their way
through the torn-up grass.

7.

Once there was a game the sisters liked to play
remembering mother at the vanity,
at five o'clock before the sun went down:
she dabbed perfume behind her ears,
in the crevice of her breasts.
The mirror lights illuminated her made-up face.
We even imitated the kiss she gave to father.

Then one day her ruby red lips,
mascara lashes, powdered cheeks
were veiled underneath black lace,
and on mother's pale face
we saw the color, like a dead light, go out.

8.

It is old,
the jade, its thick leaves clean of dust;
I remember bringing the plant home
for mother's birthday.
Widowed, she thought the years had stopped.

I see her in the kitchen
washing dishes,
her dripping hand rubbed away
steam from the plate glass.

In the window the house plants
grown over, the dark vines tangled
like the knots she cut
with scissors from our hair.

My sisters and I were outdoors
building fathers out of snow.
We left her alone for hours,
our skin raw,
holding white like warmth in our hands.
She was almost invisible
in the icy air.

9.

It was the light of day
dispersing, the white light
of my mother's skin
and the light of her love
sparkling in the snow.
From the window
I saw her playing solitaire.
I had watched her play
so many nights
from outside I could feel
each card slapped down.
There was no escape
from the rash of her loss:
it was the cold rusty
taste of snow
I licked off my mitten;
the chill down my spine
when my sister
put her snow-filled hand
under my coat,
the other sister
holding me down;
it was those long dark shadows
I believed looked after us,
gigantic in the snow.

10.

Years ago I found them
scattered like dead leaves
in a suitcase in the basement:
the pictures of my father.

I took the best ones
time hadn't reached
and opened the edges
curled like a hand.

I put them in a shoe-box,
slipped under my bed.
It was like a secret
I imagined we shared.

Eventually the tint of age
faded the images,
erased the details.
Even my hands forgot you.

BALLET LESSON

In the center
of the dance floor
my body appeared in the mirrors
around the room.
This morning
I sit on the sofa, everything
as still as those silver mirrors.
Around me the boredom of the walls,
the sun-stained Degas prints.
From the window, blades of sun
reflect other mirrors,
cut a dark patch across the room.
I stare at the light side,
a passport to the yellowed wood
my black slippers once tapped resin across,
my body neither a woman's
nor child's. A kind of marionette.
My legs as if pulled by strings
spun pirouettes:
an instrument of the body began.
I imagine the other girls in my class
dance across the room, their arms
cradling the air, tights faded, faces beams
of younger light.
I forget the usual concerns,
dust that lies captive on the wood,
the straight bind on the paperbacks
still unbroken
and listen for the count, once as constant
as the ballet teacher's drum
beating in my heart, my mind.
Now the music for the *Ronds de Jambe*,
the white-haired pianist played,
always the same chords penetrating

my school-girl dreams.
At four o'clock the lesson began.
I would watch the bare bulb
in the room, my palms wet,
legs stretched, arms opening like a fan,
the weight of my body turning
in the one discipline it understands.
The room disappears around me
until it is as damp as the dressing-room
where I unbuttoned my blouse, pulled the leotard
over my cold chest, tied my laces in.

A SISTER'S STORY

My sister startles herself from sleep.
I can feel her breath rise
in the slow-motion of mine.
I am thirteen, and she is three.

Outside sleep unravels from our bodies.
Her hand, perfect for cradling a coin,
closes within mine.
We walk in the backyard

over long grass,
between weeping willow trees.
She won't remember her dream
so I tell her another:

How a girl alone in the night,
the stars so close to her,
she takes a pair of scissors
and cuts them from the sky.

She opens her slate-colored book,
arranges the stars
into constellations,
pastes them flat as doilies.

They are like a billion
burning hearts.
Each morning the book
stretches back to the sky.

PREMONITION

I was wrapped in the darkest
part of sleep
when your cry broke through.

For a long time I lay there
waiting for mother
to cross from her room,

to lift her last born
from the fragments of your dream.
But she was hard into her sleep

where alcohol formed
its impenetrable cloud.
Inside your nursery

the air was humid
and safe
as a greenhouse.

I could see the moon
from the window
turning its back on the world.

I rocked you against my shoulder.
Sweat broke across the soft v
on the top of your forehead.

Your face was wet and warm.
The first fears
engraving your sleep.

MY MOTHER WAS A LOVER OF FLOWERS

I knew the kind that enchanted her:
a dozen weakened red and pink roses on our table.
Mother would remark *how lovely and soft*,
and bask in their aroma.
Once she was like a flower.
So beautiful that everyone wanted to know her.
Like a centerpiece, her aura said,
look, don't touch.

One autumn she brought home a bunch
of orange and yellow grotesquely shaped orchids.
Their petals resembled insects I had studied in biology.
She taught me that ugliness could be a form of beauty,
but I was afraid of it, of anything that captured her attention.
I saw what it did to one of us, her last born.

She liked to parade around our house
making sure each room was filled with flowers.
She made sure she had the right vase
so as not to clash with her bouquets;
for hours worked on her arrangements.
In the summer she loved lilacs,
in winter white roses, springtime a configuration of daisies.

Cut flowers live a short life.
Mother took them from the vase,
tied the stems with rope
and hung them upside down in a damp room
as if to preserve what she sacrificed.
That's how I learned I had no power
to stop her nature from murdering beauty.

SISTERS

Opening the door I expect to find you there
tripping the steps, thin wing of hair
sweeping behind, the color of half-ripened corn.

A welcome one dreams about, coming home from the seas or war.
This time I see you have changed.
Upstairs harboring behind your door

the way we hid together behind books,
entered worlds we hadn't known, prairies we stumbled across,
little women, petticoats, herbal recipes,

secret gardens we believed were real, red barns,
horses that could make you cry, magic, painted roads.
The dark at the end of the forest sweating in your dreams.

Now inside your rooms parcels of childhood
arrange themselves like down quilted on your bed,
I carry them in my arms while you pull away.

I'm surprised finding your face thinned, diamond white,
eyes that pool tears so much like stars, the light behind them.
Your hair, like fallen leaves, dies a little more each day;

the color is a suspension of yellow and brown.
Your small breasts float on your chest, are apple blossoms
bobbing in a pond. Your body wanders off like a shadow.

It all comes back, hurrying past every mirror,
giving in to that last trail of light, then in bed suspending
that moment in dreams of yourself, women you flip in magazines.

SISTERS

I want to make it all easy, or at least have answers
for the old body shed, for the new horrors
that arise at night, for parents quarreling,

for friends turning away and returning daily,
for desires you can't name, longings for the ease of a dream,
answers I can't give you. Reasons for surviving the night.

Reckless Heart

What the wise doubt, the fool believes—
Who is it, then, that love deceives?

Louise Bogan

THREE ON A MATCH

Summer nights we played gin rummy
in the backyard even when the mosquitoes
drove us crazy.
Our sister's hair had grown to the arch
of her back and she wore eyeliner,
black as lead, under her eyes.
As long as the lantern burned
we kept dealing the hands.
We were safe
in our protective net
of stars and constellations,
until one night she told us she was running away.
She had grown sick and tired
of the wind that ruffled the lilac bushes,
her small bedroom next to mother's
so close she could hear her breathe
through the walls,
and our childish gambling.
The night she came home
with suck bites covering her neck,
smelling of smoke and some boy,
I saw the change in her eyes,
and waited.
With one fatal sweep
she cleared away our pile of pennies,
took a twenty dollar bill
from the pocket of her jeans
and demanded we ante-up.
That's how it usually went:
she would call the game
and set the stakes,
and my younger sister and I would follow suit.

* * *

When I looked up the Big Dipper,
and the Little Dipper—
its sorry imitation—
were in the sky.

CAROUSEL

She came home drunk and laughing
with two boys from school.
I heard her footsteps coming down the stairs,
her hot breath in my ear
as she taunted me downstairs.
The night I let the other boy
feel me in the dark
my sister said it would be like heaven.
I followed down the linoleum stairs
to the damp cellar of the house.
Heaven, a place so far lost,
beyond fear and the pledge of higher virtue.
My sister twirled her long hair behind her ear,
her hoop earring
shining in the candlelight
was like the gold ring
in the center of the carousel
we all wanted to touch,
the night turning, the music pumping
faster and faster.
When I felt his hand like a cold knife
under my shirt, I watched her polished nails
close around the other boy's neck
and leave their red marks.
Her spirit over me like the canopy
of the carousel's white blinking lights
I endlessly lost myself beneath.
When the music finished and the platform
of the room stilled, I couldn't stop him;
her reckless heart was mine.

CARNIVAL

After the rain quit the carnival began.
In a rickety trolley car
we entered the Tunnel of Love.
The lawn torn up, and the dark mud.
Night destroyed the sky.
It was summer, August, the sweat was in everything.
The Laughing Lady's ceaseless laugh rang in our ears
and stayed with us like a disturbing dream.
We tunnelled further inside, into the mysterious
darkness until I no longer knew what I felt
dodging the rough turns, the moment
when we might have turned back.
All that stood before us
were white lights going round
like stars in our head after a fall.
Would the dizziness, the anxiety ever end?
Deeper and deeper we traveled
until I could no longer hear, see, feel
anyone but you.
The car came to a sudden stop—
the terrible brightness—
we had entered the world again.
As we stepped out of the car
our shoes sank in the wet, depleted earth.
The moon too had lost itself, and was pinned
mercilessly to the sky.
The pretty girl with dark roots in her bleached hair
called out to you as she raised her arm
and pointed to the stuffed animals dangling
from strings in her booth.
You carefully aimed the darts
and went after the balloons,
one after another with greater force,
blind with your purpose,

as before in the Tunnel of Love,
when you pushed into me,
the cool leather of the seat on my back,
slipped your hand under my dress
and said we were going to paradise.

RUINED SECRET

My sister fell in love
with an ex-con when she was seventeen
and swore me to secrecy.
I knew what she loved about him
the night she took me
to his run-down three family
on the dark side of a Cleveland
I'd never seen before.
On the top floor his mother lived
alone with twenty some cats
she called Sam.
From downstairs we could hear her
call the cats for dinner
and the sound of their twenty some
pairs of feet fill her kitchen.
When he heard his mother's voice
through the floorboards
he looked ashamed and lit
one of his non-filtered cigarettes
and told us the story of his brother
who was a captain in the Navy.
The smell of danger and lust
was everywhere—

in the sheets
crumpled on his bed,
in the small bathroom
wall-papered with rock stars,
the dirt underneath his nails;
his slow-tongued English of the streets.
At night my sister
talked to him on our princess phone
in the lemon-scented bedroom we shared
in whispers, and sighed at what I knew
were his hopeless declarations.

RUINED SECRET

After six months the situation had changed.
My sister refused his phone calls,
and when a dozen red roses arrived,
she dumped them in the trash out back
before mother had gotten home.
Even though months had gone by
and we stopped saying his name,
his soft darkness lived in our room
like a ruined secret.

One day he waited for her after school
in his run-down Pontiac
and she came home with her eye
bruised and a pair of garnet earrings
in her ears.

She did not know how to get rid
of what she started.
He went to his priest
to ask for salvation
and later that same day
when I was working
at the bakery counter after school
he took me by the arm,
cried, and begged *me* to forgive him.
In our bedroom we stared at the phone
waiting for the scary thrill
that pumped through our bodies
after the first ring;
but eventually the calls stopped
and I'd find my sister
staring out the window
turning the scarlet posts
on her ear that caught
the light like a bleeding heart.

STAIRWAY TO HEAVEN

My girlfriend and I snuck out
of our houses at midnight
on a Cleveland winter night
and met at the corner of our block.
Our mission was to find the two gas station
attendants we had spotted the night before.
We didn't know their names,
only their oily hands and dark coats.
Marie had big boobs and soft, Chek lips.
I was a quiet teenager with slight curves
and deep, skirting eyes.
We were a sensible team:
she was the target and I was the protection.
One boy was cuter than the other,
that's how it always went.
Marie would get in the back seat
and neck with the cute one
and I'd stay in front pressed against
the passenger door talking to the gawky driver
with a scar underneath his eye or bad teeth
above the sound of "Stairway to Heaven" or something
by Fleetwood Mac, until their lips in the back
were bruised and puffy.
Eventually, the driver pulled over
and let us out at the curb.
Marie scribbled her phone number on a matchbook.
For two or three days we'd linger near the phone
until pissed-off and pumped with revenge
we'd go out again, stalking the night
for the new replacements.
This time was my turn, I decided.
Outside the Sohio
we leaned against the unleaded
and waited for their shift to end.

When we got to the car
I slipped in the back,
ignoring Marie's tug on my sleeve.
The good one slipped in next.
The tape began: "Lucy in the Sky with Diamonds,"
joint lit, and within minutes
we were in the haze of music and drug
until we'd open the door
and let the cold blast of air rescue us.
His name was Randy.
The very minute the words slipped
from his lips I didn't want to forget him.
Randy, I thought, over and over
as he turned a lock of my hair
in his finger and began his work.
No, I *liked* the smell of petroleum
on his neck, his nicotine lips.
I could make him up in my mind
for weeks, I thought, without
knowing a single thing about him.
This time we'd wait by my phone
and when it rang I'd say, Randy,
Hello. Two words.
And the long dark dialogue
would begin.

MY GROOM

It was almost religious,
watching my groom carry out his ritual:
filling the pails with water,
coffee can with dried corn and oats
and emptying the grain into deep troughs.
I would vow to forget him
and then, not wanting to, it would happen,
I would return each year
to the open fields of Ohio
where he ran the racehorses,
the golden light of autumn
beating against their dark manes.
After the races, we'd go back to the barn
to the horses banging against their cramped stalls,
snorting and sneezing, wanting to break loose.
I watched him cool the horses down,
the flies everywhere,
my groom, his long arms taut
under his T-shirt as he carefully
brushed their backs, coaxed,
cleaned the open welts on their legs
where he'd whipped them into shape.
His fingernails were caked with mud,
long hair slicked off his forehead with sweat.
From the corner of the barn
light weakened in the slats of the roof,
bats screeched in the eaves.
When he finished he'd look at me,
standing in the shadows.
Up close, I smelled the horses,
dark and dangerous, wedded to his clothes.
His warm hands slipped down my back
underneath my shirt;
horse hooves wild as my heart

against the earth's secrets.
Is this where love begins,
in the arms of the cruel tamer,
the keeper of horses?

THE LOVER'S GIFT

Sometimes I never heard a word,
I was watching the sun
shadow in the grass,
the splinters of misgivings
I transformed to light's
brilliance in your eyes,
content with my imagining.

What kept you coming back,
your body awkward at my door?
Once you brought apples,
green, golden, and red,
their firm solidity, their skins
of bruised color.

A token of forgiveness,
I supposed,
to keep you from temptation.

Playing the lover's fool
I accepted your conceit—
with a desire more powerful than love.

Outdoors we peeled the apples,
carving the skin in one long ribbon
from the pulp.
The apple-peel swirled
against the knife.
Slowly you lifted its red dress.

THE ARTIST MISJUDGES PERFECTION

You would love to sit here.
To study the pear—
how each one is flawed
differently,
how in their imperfections
they seem perfect.
I can see you
twist one from the tree,
hold it to the sun,
the light from which all colors reflect.
"Don't, not yet,
wait, patience
my love,"
I hear you say,
always relishing the image,
as I move to take a bite.
At home you'd unwrap
the pear from your handkerchief,
shine it against the cloth of your shirt,
place it on the center of the table
for ornament,
and like a fool
who hungers only for desire,
refuse to take the knife.

A LOVER'S QUARREL

Together we went rowing.
It was April, and the lake choppy.
Soon our arms grew tired
from the constant pull of the oars
against such strong current.

We watched the ducks parade
and followed in their wake.
The males are called drakes,
and are distinguished from the females
by the green and violet bands
of color around their heads.
"Watch how they strut
across the lake," you said, smugly.

It was true.
The female ducks, crowned in dark feathers,
a camouflage to protect their young—
were huddled near a cascade of reeds and rushes.
They looked secretive and skittish.

I don't know why; it made me angry.
I let you row alone. My arms ached.
The sky went dim as though surrendering to a longing.

Eventually you gave up too,
and the current carried us to a shady bank.
For a while we just sat and listened.

A LOVER'S QUARREL

I was at another lake, far from you,
where my sisters and I used to swim naked.
Lake Erie. Even the name sent shivers down my spine.
We were so cold we formed a circle
and jumped up and down,
hair wet, skin shining,
the water holding us in such able arms.

BLUEBERRIES

Together we picked blueberries.
It was mid-August,
my hands bled from the gathering,
thumb and forefinger sore
from the pull of fruit off the branch.

That night we washed them.
Sorted the red berries from the ripe,
crushed the tiny seeds
that split from the tough, blue skin.

After we'd aired the pantry,
collected the mason jars from the cellar,
still our hands wore the color of the picking,
our bodies that ancient smell.

OH GIANT FLOWERS

Everyday I walk past the house
with the blue morning glories
covering the walls and the four sunflowers

growing in front, their tall stalks
bent over, and have to stop
and touch the dark centers

almost the size of a face.
It began the morning I awoke before you.
The blanket was wrapped tightly around you

and the sun came through the window
on your face. I couldn't stand
to see you that way. I looked outside.

The leaves red, yellow, and finishing.
A squirrel was in the yard rummaging for food
in the grass, the apple tree letting go

its bruised fruit; preparations had to be made.
How could you sleep with so much sun on your face?
When I left I didn't know where I was going.

There was so much color it seemed as if the whole
sky would ignite. The light loves the earth so much
it has to burn to prove it. Oh giant flowers,

when I came across you I wanted to bury my face
in your huge petals, I wanted to lie down
in the grass beneath you.

A LOVER'S PLEA

I am lost and already it is dusk.
How will I find my way to your house
if there is no light to guide me?

All afternoon I watched one purple flower
close up to the cold like a child.
I stood underneath the magnificent tree.

Those long limbs draped their yellow and gold before me.
In the fallen leaves crushed now to the ground
is the one red leaf I have prayed for.

WITHOUT

Why does the woman lay her head so far
against her shoulder, why the still smile?
Her blouse only covers one of her breasts
and her plump arms are milky white.
Perhaps she has just made love, dressed,
and moved to the red chair after her lover
has left. Her hands are placed
over her crotch but it is not pain that draws
her face, or if so, pain cut small by pleasure.
In the hour after she held on to him the way
she must have been held as a young girl
before she had begun to bleed.
Already one side of her face is darkening.
Later she might cut her yellow hair.
She is without her lover and her father
is far away. Her face is the halves of a heart.

IRONING

The girl is ironing in the small
light left after dusk.
Her head tilted over the board,
her long red hair almost catching in the iron.
She sprinkles water from a blue bowl
onto a printed shirt.
Light steam slowly escapes.
Already her eyes look older.
She remembers as a child watching her mother
pressing the sheets. She helped fold them,
asking questions one after another,
listening to the sound of her mother's voice.
All that mattered was that the sheets
were cold and crisp when she slipped into bed
and smelled like the wind that blew them dry.
Now she slides the iron down the back of the shirt and yawns.
She belongs to no one.

GRIEF

Almost dawn,
the girl sits at the table
by the window
tracing the patterns
on the lace cloth with her fingers.

As the kitchen slowly brightens
she begins to see the petals
on the floral papered walls.
So much of what she feels
never leaves this room.

Winter

The difference between Despair
And Fear—is like the One
Between the instant of a Wreck—
And when the Wreck has been—

Emily Dickinson

WHAT YOU ARE
LEFT WITH

When the summer leaves
it takes some light

with it. Some birds go
too. All the windows

have to be closed.
The cold comes

and you live with it.
The trees lose

their leaves but
the branches are still strong

and suffice. The wind goes
on. But in your mind

you still hold the birds,
the green grass

and the red tomatoes
weighing down the vine.

SKATING POND

The grey sky gives over
and the dark starlings gather
in one otherwise empty tree.
The bleachers are cold.

No one is skating
but deep scratches
are gouged in the ice.

It is enough to look out
past the pond where certain trees
and houses alter
simply by the raw snow
falling in the January light.

The sun spreads itself to nothing
and the day holds on
to what little is left.
And because you don't know
what you want, all of it matters.

COLD HEART

The slow drift of clouds
neglects the face of the sun,
and the snow keeps coming.

The less than tame wind dismantles it,
brushes the black branches
of a particular oak to one side
like a girl throwing back her hair.
The ice engraved in the crevices
of bark is your idea of sensual.

You would find it more than beautiful,
this wilderness where a pine
is the only thing in sight, green, unstripped.
Only you'd be obsessed with the lesser,
barer trees, how immense you'd feel
next to them, how gracious you'd become,

and the starlings, how they regroup
from tree to tree in one thick flock,
how they leave not one alone.
Sometimes the wind gets so crazy
and goes on for so long,
as though confessing

to the air. You would stand still and listen,
note how the dry falling snow
dies into the rest of itself,
and for a minute your cold heart

would quiver. I wish you could see
each morning the red-headed woodpecker
knocking against the bark,
how safe he is from all reasoning.

SNOW FALLING UPSIDE DOWN

The sound of the chamber organ
came into my life
the way the snow might have fallen
over a red glove I found one March morning
when everything had begun to thaw.

Two or three stars
broke the complete
sky and the brave ash stood
silvered and still in the loneliness
of the air.

The wind sighed its long
regret against the window
of the thrift shop—
the music's crescendo
falling over the antique doll
no one could hold,

and beside her the paperweight,
where a snowman inside a globe
holds a yellow balloon in his hand.
If you turned the globe upside down
it was as if his world were breaking apart,
and the balloon, like a lost heart
in the snow, eventually drifted away.

HOUSE CAT

The heart of patience
lives in a room
where the faded carpet suffers
from the sunlight coming in,
the violet nightgown
hangs formless on the hook by the bed,
and the silk rose in the clear
vase on the pine dresser
is covered with dust.

And yet, still
day after day she hungers
for the wet oak
and its elaborate configuration
of branches from the window.

CHILDBIRTH, 1943

In memory of my grandmother, Lillian Greenbaum

1.

July. The darkness hints
at the edges of counters, the kitchen
warm with the smell of a summer storm.
The grown-ups talk in low voices.
The young girl's father sits near the window
watching drops of rain arrange
themselves along the glass.

2.

December.
The snow
begins
to build.
The girl
takes a handful
and molds it
until it is hard
enough to throw.
The voice
of the wind
is like the eerie
sound
inside the walls
of the house
where for weeks now
her mother lies in bed.

CHILDBIRTH, 1943

3.

The young girl presses her ear
against her mother's belly.
Inside a child is slowly taking form.
The girl lifts her head to her mother's chest.
She feels the hushed syllables
of her mother's breath kiss the arch of her neck.

Outside the snow begins to drift.
The girl's father takes the shovel,
plunges it into the earth,
as if he were preparing
and looks to the sky
filled with darting snow.

4.

In her sleep
the girl hears the whistle of the kettle.
it steams and steams
with the desire to go on forever.

She finds her mother in the bathroom,
her arms propped against the sink,
her head resting in her arms.
The girl looks inside the sink
at the yellow stains
and the water drops around the drain.
With her hand she pulls back her mother's hair.

5.

When it is time
the grass is stiff
with frozen snow.
From the doorway
the girl hears
her parents' footsteps
crunch the frozen ground.

She stands
in a pair
of her mother's footprints
until her grandparents
call to shelter her inside.

The month is April,
when something is born, and taken,
when warm air turns up rotted grass
and trees begin to blossom.

The young girl is in her room,
beside the window
covered with a sun-cracked shade.
At night she fingers the hollow space
in her doll's chest
where the heart should be
and remembers her mother.

HISTORY LESSON

This is the way we learn history:
how each grass blade breathes
until the entire lawn shifts,
or the way we remember a certain friend
by the way she tore leaves from trees,
or our mother rubbing silver
for the table at dusk.

Last night over coffee
my friend's voice defined regret,
he no longer spoke with his hands.
He said sadness was the way
autumn trees gave up their leaves
as he watched the movers stack boxes
outside his parents' home;
how his father never forgave him
for refusing to go to war.

The year I turned thirteen
I couldn't stand any of them.
Once a year we used to gather for the holiday
around grandmother's table,
my mother, sisters, aunts, uncles, cousins;
It was the taste of challah, soft and doughy
that I remember.
The dining-room was too hot;
my grandfather ate with his fork turned around;
grandmother's wet kisses.

All that day, like a fool
I thought it was possible to disown my family.
I listened impatiently to the story
of how my great-grandmother in Russia
braided bread for the evening meal,

lit candles, softened the white flame with her hands
and whispered the ancient prayer for bread,
dark wine, for all of us, even the unborn.

SILVER

On the butcher block table
is the silver that has been housed
in a molded cardboard box in mother's basement
and handed down to me as my inheritance.
It was great grandmother's silver;
she died in Russia before I was born.
From great grandmother's table
this silver came to rest in another
drawer in the cherry bureau
of her daughter's house in Cleveland.

It came to me as I began my work.
This silver had been set, and washed,
and laid down again, night after night,
with bowls of borscht, roasted potatoes,
brisket so tender it could be cut with a fork,
in the evening candlelight after the Sabbath.
It was this butter knife
my father held in his hand, and raised
against his father in anger.
This fork he eagerly
brought to his lips
as he listened to the hushed talk
of babies lost and relatives killed in the war.

It took all day to polish the servings for twelve,
the salt and pepper shakers, sugar bowl, and creamer
all wearing the monogrammed inscription
of the family initial.
Afterwards I was tired.
I looked at my days work spread out on the butcher block,
sparkling against the last stain of sun

SILVER

the way one might come upon
a dark family secret
rubbed out after a month;
a year, a decade of tarnish.

THE DAY THE WORLD
STOPPED

The day the world stopped
I was lying on my bed
on a muggy Saturday afternoon.
The wind so still it was as if the world,
like a baby born too soon, had just taken its last breath.

In the house next door someone's mother
was chopping onions and cabbage for slaw.
Was it for a picnic at the lake,
a family barbecue?
From the house behind us
I could hear our neighbor working on his car,
the sound of each tool as it hit the hot pavement.

I have always admired the art of keeping house,
the clickety-clack of dishes being stacked,
the growl of the garbage disposal sucking up
the last trace of a graceful dinner
labored over all day.
The ordinary rhythms of a house
untouched by anguish.

It was so quiet
you could hear the sprinklers on the lawn
roll in their perfect arcs.
If there is a sound the heart makes when it breaks
it wasn't heard.

THE END OF DESIRE

When I was a child
I used to love to stare at lovers—
at couples kissing, a man looking
longingly into a woman's eyes,
a woman adoring back
and marvel over the possibilities of love.
Usually I was with my sister,
standing in a grocery line,
or outside a theater.
She would tug at my sleeve,
roll her eyes and banish me with her words:
"Stop staring! What's wrong with you!"
I *did* feel that something was wrong—
that I could be so content absorbing
the wave of her hair, the scent of perfume,
his strong fingers cupped around her shoulder.
It was the long, uninterrupted gaze I most preferred.
At the movies, I would draw into myself
as I watched on the big screen lovers kiss
and felt a stab of pain in the center of my stomach
travel through my body like a drug—
and for that brief time it was as though
I was the lover, the receiver of such rapt attention.
When the lights came on I carried the kiss
with me all through the rest of the late afternoon,
through the long walk home underneath the autumn arbors,
through the dull and tedious routine of dinner,
until I was alone in my bedroom and could replay
the scene in my mind without interruption.
I knew that as long as I was allowed to look,
to linger, to stare,
to become one with that spell that was so other,
to know and then to have—
that one day, my desire would end.

BALTIMORE,
ON TURNING THIRTY-SEVEN

For Kendra

From the third floor bay window
in a row house on North Calvert
I saw the lights go out

in your apartment across the street
still too high
from the intensity of nicotine,

and in trouble
with my live-in boyfriend
for coming home so late, to sleep.

In the shadow of a curtain
I saw the faint light of a candle.
A boy embrace you in the doorway.

Now we are both married
and live in different cities.
If we're lucky, we see each other once a year.

On this overnight visit
we have dinner at Alonso's.
After ten years

the green leather booths
have shown their age, and yet,
even the way the salt and pepper shakers,

mustard and ketchup are arranged
are as familiar as the gesture
of your hand.

Later the house is quiet.
Husband and child
asleep upstairs.

My husband is so far away
I feel as if I barely know him.
Who is he to me now that our bodies are apart?

At the breakfast table
I study your daughter as she eats her cereal
and see your serious look in her face.

How your curiosity for bugs, frogs,
and hamsters delight her.
Your husband has left early for work.

I feel wicked.   Tired.   Stolen.
As the train moves out of the station
I watch the snow fall thick

on the roofs of warehouses and schoolyards,
grow intense as a furious wind,
threaten to white-out,

diminish, pick up again.
We cannot predict
when or why or how it will engage us.

The phone lines are heavy.
Connections buried again.
A hungry bird calls out in the winter white.

A feeling takes hold,
freezes and thaws
like water into ice.

The body
has its own language, like a braille.
We do not own it, nor offer it, nor possess it.

As snow continues to thrash
against the crippled trees
the sound of loss

canvasses the landscape.
Already I long for tonight.
I imagine my husband making dinner

in our half-finished kitchen.
Our faded favorite chair.
How quickly his presence will absorb me.

How the stars in the dark sky
will fail to disappoint.
The train moves.

The earth is winded.
The snow blurs with sky.
Our lives are drawn as simply

and haphazardly as a child
dragging a stick along the snow,
leaving a trail of x's.

A bird calls out again.
A wrenching cry.
The train pulls me forward.

THE DROWNING

It isn't human not to struggle
underwater

not to want to breathe.
Yesterday at our neighbor's pool

you forced my head underwater,
a game to see who could stay under longest,

who could suffer longer.
When I started to rise up for air

you pulled my shoulders down,
wanting to see me struggle.

My legs and arms flailed,
then instinctively

I kicked you until I surfaced.
At night you reach for me

in our bed,
slide into my back,

brush your lips
against my forehead, eyes, face

as if you've *really* saved me,
and are overcome with remorse

for what you nearly lost,
a tenderness a small child,

a woman who has not been loved
in years, a damaged sister,

would covet.
Harder, I say, *be mean.*

The way I learned to love
was to give, to be kind, patient,

to be not someone to fight for.
When I close my eyes

I'm still floating
face down

waiting for you
to breathe air into my lungs.

What I want is to defy
my nature.

Stronger, I say.
Make it stop,

the desire.
Hurt me, I say, *harder.*

THE RUNAWAY

On a summer day full of promise
we piled into my mother's car
and drove my youngest sister
to camp for the summer.

That night she ran away
and called from a stranger's
house to beg our mother
to bring her home.

Years later,
she took the keys
to my mother's white Saab,
closed the garage door
and turned on the ignition.

On a day less remembered
for the violent rain
than for how little was the same as before,
the sky closed its eyes on our house
as if in shame and claimed her.

THE SUICIDE'S GARDEN

In her garden
tall and sleek roses grow decadently

for the shears, and for our pleasure.

Look how lovely
the fresh cut roses on my table.

Their life so short,
and yet no less beautiful

or real, than the roses
on the vines in the garden.

How willingly the tender
prepares the earth for beauty's sake:

as if he were the master of her execution.

THE GODDESS OF DESPAIR

Against such cold and mercurial mornings,
watch the wind whirl one leaf
across the landscape,
then in a breath, let it go.
 The color in the opaque sky
seems almost not to exist.

Put on a wool sweater.
Wander in the leaves,
underneath healthy elms.
Hold your child in your arms.

After the dishes are washed,
a kiss still warm at your neck,
put down your pen. Turn out the light.

I know how difficult it is,
always balancing and weighing,
it takes years and many transformations;
and always another loss to stop for,

to send you backwards.

Why do you worry so,
when none of us is spared?

STOLEN CRY

I awoke at two a.m.
and looked out the bay windows
as the pregnant sky gradually came to life.

From the backdrop of weathered buildings
I heard a cry in the night.
The sound of something injured.
The nursery was empty.

A greedy lover,
to give to his betrothed,
had robbed us of what was promised.

AMERICAN LANDSCAPE

The tern dives headfirst into the sea,
catches a fish, soars again, takes another dive.
There is not a rusted can, cigarette butt,
Big Mac wrapper on the beach.
The ocean stretches like a canvas
to the edge of the pale pastels of this artificial
mini beach town city designed by an architect
I heard Prince Charles had praised.

Modern steel sculptures in the shape of sea birds
appear to have landed on front lawns,
hand-painted Santa Fe style furniture sits in living rooms
dotted swiss curtains and frilly fabrics
mimic scenes from story-books.
In this American city ten years old
everything is pre-arranged, pre-fabricated.
City planners and architects have come to study it.
I hear they are planning one in Maryland.

The beach is dotted with the delicate
thread-work of nests like clumps of tangled hair
and wears the imprint of the sandpipers,
their bellies the color of sand.
The baby sandpipers have hatched.
In the air is the sound of their squeaking.
The monarchs have magically emerged from their cocoons.
There is no sign of humanity in sight.

It is like a ghost town now that it is October
and the second-home residents have migrated
back to their homes in Alabama, Missouri, Georgia.
I walk the Seaside, Florida streets
reading the names of the houses—
Châtelet, Peek-a-boo, Blue Moon.
One of the twenty-six year round residents
remarked that in this town the gossip
is about other people's houses.

THE DAWN OF THE END
OF CIVILIZATION

I carry the image like a treasured snapshot:
a lovely man dressed in a soft, faded sweatshirt,
blue jeans, pair of flip-flops, carries his two year old red-head
boy in his arms across the small sand-pebbled roads
in a Disneyland-like town, Seaside, Florida,
where the houses are all pastels; on the last day of October,
headed toward the windy surf of a desolate beach
where only the rich have worn the shores barefoot
on sand fine as baby powder.
My boy would have been a red-head.

It was the eve of the first of November.
There was absolutely no sun. No chance.
Barely a slice of blue in the white opaque sky.
There was good food—salmon peppered and grilled.
Complicated conversation.
Later I walked the beach and shooed away flies.
The seductive, dangerous curl of the waves threatened to shake it,
but the image stayed with me. It was the dawn of the day
I would never give birth to; the life I would never have.

I was afraid.

NOTES AND ACKNOWLEDGMENTS

Epigraph to *The End of Desire*: from "Thirteen Ways of Looking at a Blackbird" by Wallace Stevens. Acknowledgment is made to Alfred A. Knopf, Inc., New York, and Faber and Faber Limited, London for permission to reprint an excerpt from "Thirteen Ways of Looking at a Blackbird" from *The Collected Poems* of Wallace Stevens, copyright 1923, copyright renewed 1951 by Wallace Stevens.

Epigraph to "The House": from "Ariel" by Sylvia Plath

Epigraph to "Reckless Heart": from "Juan's Song" by Louise Bogan

Epigraph to "Winter": Poem #305 from *The Complete Poems of Emily Dickinson* is reprinted courtesy of Little, Brown and Company, Boston.

"Without" is a response to the painting, "The Dream," by Pablo Picasso, 1932

"Ironing" is a response to the painting, "A Woman Ironing," by Pablo Picasso, 1901

Many thanks to Yaddo Corporation for the Arts, Ragdale Foundation, and Virginia Center for the Creative Arts for their support; to Eavan Boland and Harriet Levin for their generous comments; and to Harry Ford for his encouragement.

A NOTE ABOUT THE AUTHOR

Jill Bialosky was born in Cleveland, Ohio. She studied at Ohio University and received a Master of Arts degree from the Writing Seminars at The Johns Hopkins University, and a Master of Fine Arts degree from The University of Iowa's Writer's Workshop. Her poems have been published in many magazines, including *Partisan Review* and *TriQuarterly*, and have received a number of awards. She is currently an editor at W. W. Norton & Company and lives in New York City.

A NOTE ON THE TYPE

This book was set on the Linotype in Monticello, a revival of the original Roman No. 1 cut by Archibald Binny and cast in 1796 by the Philadelphia type foundry Binny & Ronaldson. The face was named Monticello in honor of its use in the fifty-volume *Papers of Thomas Jefferson*, published by Princeton University Press. Monticello is a transitional type design, embodying certain features of Bulmer and Baskerville, but it is a distinguished face in its own right.

Composition by Heritage Printers, Inc., Charlotte, N.C.
Printed and bound by Quebecor Printing, Kingsport, Tennessee
Designed by Harry Ford